SESAME STREET®

TOUGH TOPICS

Talking about

Natural Disasters

A Sesame Street
Resource

Marie-Therese Miller

Lerner Publications ◆ Minneapolis

Dear Grown-Up,

The more comfortable you are talking with children about the challenges they face, the more of a difference you can make in their lives. In this series, *Sesame Street* friends provide caregivers and educators a starting point to discuss, process, and offer support on tough topics. Together, we can help kids learn coping and resilience-building techniques to help them face tough challenges such as divorce, grief, and more.

Sincerely,
the Editors at Sesame Workshop

Table of Contents

What Are Natural Disasters?

Natural disasters, like hurricanes, tornadoes, and earthquakes, sometimes happen. They can be sudden and scary.

Being prepared and learning about natural disasters can help.

Hurricanes have strong winds and lots of rain.

Tornadoes are spinning columns of air that look like funnels or tubes. Sometimes they're called twisters!

You might need to go to a safer place.

If the lights go out, you can use a flashlight.

Winter storms can bring lots of snow and wind. To stay safe, you might stay inside with your family. You will be cozy together.

Wildfires are fires that start outside in forests or prairies.

Firefighters are there to help! They know what to do, so it's important to listen to them.

Earthquakes make the ground shake.

Floods happen when a lot of water comes onto dry land. Often it's because there is too much rain.

If I feel scared, I talk to my mommy.

Be Prepared

It's important to be prepared for a natural disaster. Talk with your family about your emergency plan so everyone will know what to do.

You can make an emergency kit together. You can add canned food and a can opener, water, flashlights, batteries, first aid supplies, and blankets.

I added a coloring book, crayons, some games, my teddy bear Radar, and birdseed to my emergency kit.

Practice your first and last name, your grown-ups' names, your address, and your grown-ups' phone numbers. These are good to know in emergencies.

My name is Rosita de las Cuevas.
My parents are Ricardo and Rosa.
My address is 123 Sesame Street.

There are many kinds of helpers during a natural disaster, like firefighters and paramedics.

Sometimes people go to a shelter to be safe. Volunteers give warm blankets, water, and food.

Be a good listener during a natural disaster.
Helpers will tell everyone what to do.

It is important to stay with your family or other safe grown-ups.

You can be a helper by listening.

Now you know more about natural disasters and how to be prepared. Remember that there are many people to help keep you safe!

Helpers are our friends!

What You Can Do

1. Make an emergency plan.

2. Create an emergency kit.

3. Practice your name, your grown ups' names, your address, and your grown-ups' phone numbers.

4. Look for the helpers.

5. Listen to grown-ups you trust.

6. If you're feeling nervous or worried, try belly breathing.

Belly breathing can help you feel calm. Put your hands on your belly. Now slowly breathe in through your nose and then slowly breathe out through your mouth. Try it three more times. After belly breathing, you might feel more relaxed.

Glossary

emergency kit: supplies needed to be prepared for a natural disaster

firefighters: helpers who put out fires and keep people safe

hurricanes: large, windy storms that form over oceans

paramedics: helpers who take care of sick or injured people

prairies: big stretches of land with lots of grass and not many trees

Read More

Boothroyd, Jennifer. *All about Firefighters*. Minneapolis: Lerner Publications, 2021.

Kesselring, Susan. *Weather Safety*. New York: AV2 by Weigl, 2020.

Meinking, Mary. *Natural Disasters*. Minneapolis: Cody Koala, 2019.

Explore more resources that help kids (and their grown-ups!) provided by Sesame Workshop, the nonprofit educational organization behind Sesame Street. Visit https://sesameworkshop.org/tough-topics/.

Photo Acknowledgments

Image credits: SerrNovik/Getty Images, p. 4; Warren Faidley/Getty Images, p. 6; Francis Lavigne-Theriault/Getty Images, p. 7; YinYang/Getty Images, p. 8; John Callahan/Getty Images, p. 9; Jeff Miller/Getty Images, p. 10; AwakenedEye/Getty Images, p. 11; David Pereiras/Shutterstock, p. 12; d3sign/Getty Images, p. 14; gorodenkoff/Getty Images, p. 16 (top, center); egon69/Getty Images, p. 16 (lower); FG Trade/Getty Images, p. 17; shironosov/Getty Images, p. 18; kali9/Getty Images, p. 21.

Cover: Warren Faidley/Getty Images.

Index

Lerner Publishing Group, Inc. produced this book with help from the Federal Emergency Management Agency (FEMA). Go to Ready.gov or Ready.gov/kids for more information.

To FEMA for its generous review of this book and to all the helpers who respond to natural disasters

Lerner Publications Company
An imprint of Lerner Publishing Group, Inc.
241 First Avenue North
Minneapolis, MN 55401 USA

For reading levels and more information, look up this title at www.lernerbooks.com.

Main body text set in Mikado. Typeface provided by HVD.

Editor: Amber Ross **Designer:** Laura Otto Rinne
Photo Editor: Cynthia Zemlicka
Lerner team: Martha Kranes

Library of Congress Cataloging-in-Publication Data

Names: Miller, Marie-Therese, author.
Title: Talking about natural disasters : a Sesame Street resource / Marie-Therese Miller.
Description: Minneapolis : Lerner Publications, [2025] | Series: Sesame Street tough topics | Includes bibliographical references and index. | Audience: Ages 4–8 | Audience: Grades K–1 | Summary: "Natural disasters such as hurricanes, wildfires, or floods can be scary. Sesame Street friends invite young readers to make an emergency plan and remind them that there are people to help when disaster strikes"— Provided by publisher.
Identifiers: LCCN 2023031851 (print) | LCCN 2023031852 (ebook) | ISBN 9798765620199 (library binding) | ISBN 9798765629710 (paperback) | ISBN 9798765637524 (epub)
Subjects: LCSH: Natural disasters—Juvenile literature.
Classification: LCC GB5019 .M57 2025 (print) | LCC GB5019 (ebook) | DDC 363.34/7—dc23/eng20230926

LC record available at https://lccn.loc.gov/2023031851
LC ebook record available at https://lccn.loc.gov/2023031852

Manufactured in the United States of America
1-1009963-51824-9/28/2023